OTHER HELEN EXLEY GIFTBOOKS:

I love you madly
The Bride
Words on Love & Romance
A Special Gift – My Wishes For You

Published simultaneously in 2006 by Helen Exley Giftbooks Ltd in Great Britain,
and Helen Exley Giftbooks LLC in the USA.

ILLUSTRATIONS BY JULIETTE CLARKE

2 4 6 8 10 12 11 9 7 5 3 1

Illustrations copyright © Helen Exley 2006.
Selection and arrangement copyright © Helen Exley 2006.
The moral right of the author has been asserted.

ISBN 1-905130-03-1

Words and pictures selected by Helen Exley.
Printed in China.

Helen Exley Giftbooks Ltd, 16 Chalk Hill, Watford, Herts WD19 4BG, UK
Helen Exley Giftbooks LLC, 185 Main Street, Spencer, MA 01562, USA
www.helenexleygiftbooks.com

THE
GREAT GIFT
of
LOVE

A HELEN EXLEY GIFTBOOK

yours is the grace

Yours is the breath that sets every new leaf a-quiver.
Yours is the grace that guides the rush of the river.
Yours is the flush and the flame in the heart of a flower:
Life's meaning, its music, its pride and its power.

ANONYMOUS, FROM "YOU"

because of you

My feet shall run because of you
My feet dance because of you
My heart shall beat because of you
My eyes see because of you
My mind thinks because of you
And I shall love because of you.

ESKIMO LOVE SONG

LOVE COMES AND TOUCHES YOU

...UNDER THE SUMMER ROSES,

WHEN THE FRAGRANT CRIMSON

LURKS IN THE DUSK

OF THE WILD RED LEAVES,

LOVE, WITH LITTLE HANDS,

COMES AND TOUCHES YOU

WITH A THOUSAND MEMORIES

AND ASKS YOU

BEAUTIFUL, UNANSWERABLE QUESTIONS.

CARL SANDBURG (1878-1967)

There is nothing holier,
in this life of ours,
than the first conciousness of love –
the first fluttering
of its silken wings.

HENRY WADSWORTH LONGFELLOW
(1807-1882)

Raise me a dais of silk and down;
Hang it with vair and purple dyes;
Carve it in doves, and pomegranates,
And peacocks with a hundred eyes;
Work it in gold and silver grapes.
In leaves, and silver fleurs-de-lys;
Because the birthday of my life
Is come, my love is come to me.

CHRISTINA ROSSETTI (1830-1894)

Love wakes us,
once a lifetime each.

COVENTRY PATMORE (1823-1896),
FROM "THE REVELATION"

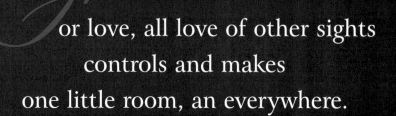

For love, all love of other sights
controls and makes
one little room, an everywhere.

JOHN DONNE
(1572-1631),
FROM "THE GOOD MORROW"

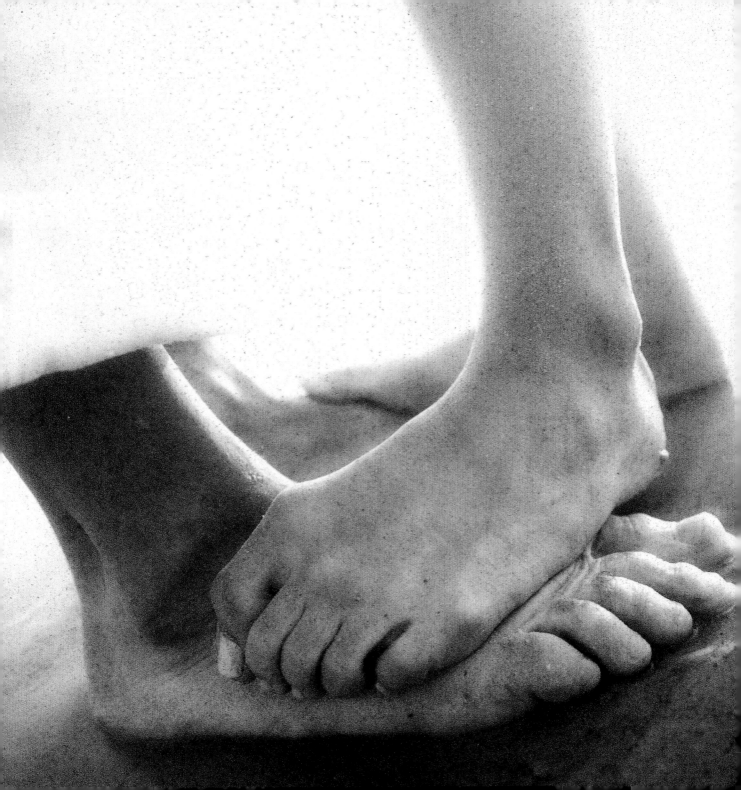

all things in love

The whole world
is a market-place for Love,
For naught that is,
from Love remains remote.
The Eternal Wisdom
made all things in Love.

FARID AL DIN ATTAR

*O*h, what a dear ravishing thing
is the beginning of an Amour!

APHRA BEHN (1640-1689)

...the world was newly crowned
with flowers, when first we met.

THOMAS HOOD (1799-1845),
FROM "THE TIME OF ROSES"

Love is the May-day

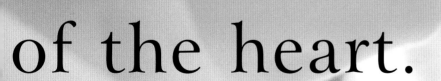

of the heart.

BENJAMIN DISRAELI (1804-1881)

"No thoroughfare"

Across the gateway of my heart
I wrote, "No thoroughfare."
But love came laughing by and cried,
"I enter everywhere."

HERBERT SHIPMAN

...No one knows
how it is that with one glance
a boy can break through
into a girl's heart.

NANCY THAYER

Our meeting makes this summer night
A new world, with new species and new dangers;
And we are made new in each other's sight....

JAMES MCAULEY (1917-1976)

SHOSHONE LOVE SONG

Fair is the white star of twilight,
and the sky clearer
At the day's end;
But she is fairer, and she is dearer,
She, my heart's friend!

Fair is the white star of twilight,
And the moon roving
To the sky's end;
But she is fairer, better worth loving,
She, my heart's friend.

It takes a lot
of courage
to show
your dreams
to someone
else.

ERMA BOMBECK (1927-1996)

the long wilderness

It seems to me, to myself,

that no man was ever before to any woman

what you are to me –

only I know what was behind –

the long wilderness

without the blossoming rose...

and the capacity for happiness,

like a black gaping hole,

before this silver flooding.

ELIZABETH BARRETT BROWNING (1806-1861),
TO ROBERT BROWNING (1812-1889)

...for two days, I have been asking myself
every moment if such happiness
is not a dream. It seems to me that what
I feel is not of earth. I cannot yet
comprehend this cloudless heaven.

VICTOR HUGO (1802-1855), TO ADÈLE FOUCHER

*Love will make a way
out of no way*

If it is your time love will track you down
like a cruise missile. If you say
"No! I don't want it right now,"
that's when you'll get it for sure.
Love will make a way out of no way.

LYNDA BARRY, FROM "BIG IDEAS"

Love is supposed to be as effortless as breathing
and as lovely as fallen snow – and it is.

JULIE KRONE, B.1963

YOU CAME

...You came, and the sun came after,
And the green grew golden above;
And the flag-flowers lightened with laughter,
And the meadow-sweet shook with love.

ALGERNON CHARLES SWINBURNE
(1837-1909),
FROM "AN INTERLUDE"

...Falling in love...
is a simultaneous firing
of two spirits....
And the sensation
is of something having
noiselessly exploded
inside each of them.

LAWRENCE DURRELL (1912-1990)

That is the true season
of love, when we believe
that we alone can love,
that no one could ever
have loved so before us,
and no one will love
in the same way after us.

JOHANN WOLFGANG VON GOETHE
(1749-1832)

so delicate

Love is... a flower so delicate that a touch will bruise it, so strong that nothing will stop its growth.

FERN WHEELER

Love is the strongest force
the world possesses,
and yet it is the humblest imaginable.

MOHANDAS K. GANDHI (1869-1948)

Our love is like the misty rain
that falls softly –
but floods the river.

AFRICAN PROVERB

The end of my heart

...I was at a party feeling very shy
because there were a lot of celebrities around,
and I was sitting in a corner alone
and a very beautiful young man came up to me
and offered me some salted peanuts
and he said, "I wish they were emeralds"
as he handed me the peanuts
and that was the end of my heart.
I never got it back.

HELEN HAYES
(1900-1993),
ON FIRST MEETING HER HUSBAND,
CHARLES MACARTHUR

*L*ove from one being to another
can only be that two solitudes
come nearer, recognize and protect
and comfort each other.

HAN SUYIN
(ELIZABETH COMBER),
B.1917

Intoxicated by
the Wine of Love

The Eternal Wisdom made all things in Love:
On Love all depend, to Love all turn.
The earth, the heavens, the sun, the moon, the stars
The centre of their orbit all find in Love.
By Love all are bewildered, stupefied,
Intoxicated by the Wine of Love.

FARID AL-DIN ATTAR

love gives a new perception

Leaves are flung from crevices of stone,
Butterflies dart among the purple blossoms,
rooted in soot-saturated brick.
Puddles shine,
and starlings swirl above the traffic.
Even the traffic lights are magical.

PAM BROWN, B.1928

*L*ove, supreme power of the heart,
mysterious enthusiasm that encloses in itself
all poetry, all heroism, all religion!

GERMAINE DE STAËL (1766-1817),
FROM "DELPHINE"

Supreme power of the heart

LOVE is a wizard.
It intoxicates, it envelops,
it isolates.
It creates fragrance
in the air,
ardor from coldness,
it beautifies
everything around it.

LEOS JANACEK (1854-1928)

Amid the gloom and travail of existence suddenly to feel
an overwhelming conviction that our destiny must be entwined;
that there is no more joy than in her joy, no sorrow but when
she grieves; that in her sigh of love, in her smile of fondness,
hereafter is all bliss; to feel our flaunty ambition fade away
all former hopes, ties, schemes, views; to violate in her favour
every duty of society; this is a lover, and this is love.

BENJAMIN DISRAELI (1804-1881), FROM "HENRIETTA TEMPLE"

I seem to have loved you
in numberless forms,
numberless times,
In life after life,
in age after age forever.
My spell-bound heart
has made and
re-made the necklace
of songs
That you take as a gift,
wear round your neck
in your many forms
In life after life,
in age after age forever.

Whenever I hear old
chronicles of love,
its age-old pain,
Its ancient tale of being apart
or together,
As I stare on and on into the past,
in the end you emerge
Clad in the light
of a pole-star
piercing the darkness of time:
You become an image
of what is remembered forever.

RABINDRANATH TAGORE
(1861-1941),
EXTRACT FROM
"UNENDING LOVE"

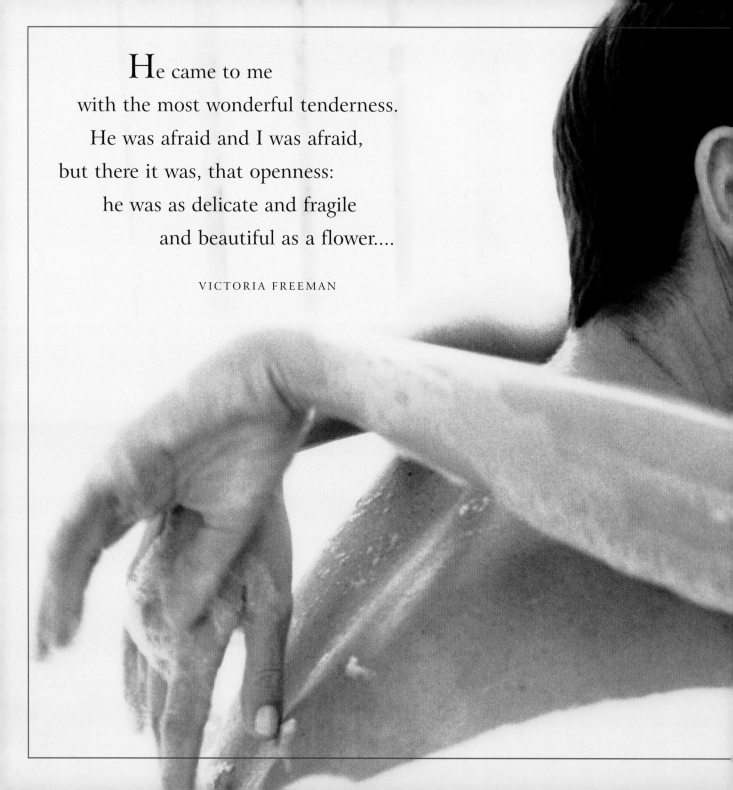

He came to me
with the most wonderful tenderness.
He was afraid and I was afraid,
but there it was, that openness:
he was as delicate and fragile
and beautiful as a flower....

VICTORIA FREEMAN

A sunbeam filtering through the blind shed a gentle light on her soft golden hair, on her pure throat, on her tranquil breast... it seemed to me that I had known her for a long time, and that before her I had known nothing and had not lived.... "And here I am sitting opposite her," I was thinking, "I have met her; I know her. God, what happiness!" I almost leapt from my chair in ecstasy....

IVAN TURGENEV (1818-1883),
FROM "FIRST LOVE"

my inmost being...

....*M*y life, my dear sweet life,
my life-light, my all,
my goods and chattels, my castles,
acres, lawns and vineyards,
O sun of my life, sun, moon, and stars,
heaven and earth, my past and future,
my bride, my girl, my dear friend,
my inmost being....

HEINRICH VON KLEIST
(1777-1811),
TO ADOLFINE HENRIETTE VOGEL

Love is a taste of paradise.

SHOLOM ALEICHEM (1859-1916)

Love can tell,

Whence the million

Why each atom

How in spite

Gay is life, and

and love alone,

stars were strewn,

knows its own,

of woe and death,

sweet is breath.

ROBERT BRIDGES (1844-1930),
FROM "MY DELIGHT AND THY DELIGHT"

WE ARE MADE FOR LOVING;
ALL THE SWEETS OF LIVING ARE
FOR THOSE THAT LOVE.
BE JOYFUL, UNAFRAID.

THE RUBAIYAT OF OMAR KHAYAM
(C.1048-C.1122)

Come to me
Not as a river willingly downward falls
To be lost in a wide ocean.
But come to me
As flood-time comes to shoreline
Filling empty bays
With a white stillness
Mating earth and sea.

ANNE WILKINSON,
FROM "IN JUNE AND GENTLE OVEN"

...their souls kissed,
they kissed with their eyes,
they were both but one single kiss.

HEINRICH HEINE (1797-1856)

Love me

Love me
with thine hand
    stretched out
Freely –
    open-minded.

ELIZABETH BARRETT BROWNING
(1806-1861)

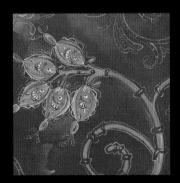

LAST NIGHT
WHEN
I THOUGHT
OF YOU
ALL THE DESERTS
BECAME
FRAGRANT
WITH ZEPHYRS.
SPRING
WAS EVERYWHERE
AND
MY DYING HEART
SUDDENLY
CAME BACK
TO LIFE.

FAIZ AHMED FAIZ

QUIETLY IN EACH OTHER'S ARMS

He carried her to the window,
so that she, too, saw the view.
They sank upon their knees,
invisible from the road,
they hoped, and began
to whisper one another's names.
Ah! It was worthwhile;
it was the great joy
that they had expected,

and countless little joys
of which they had never dreamt....
Then they spoke of other things –
the desultory talk
of those who have been fighting
to reach one another,
and whose reward is to rest
quietly in each other's arms.

E.M. FORSTER (1879-1970), FROM "A ROOM WITH A VIEW"

like stealing fire
from heaven

TO LOVE ONE WHO LOVES YOU…
TO BE THE IDOL; OF ONE'S IDOL;
IS EXCEEDING THE LIMIT OF HUMAN JOY;
IT IS STEALING FIRE FROM HEAVEN.

DAPHINE DE GIRARDIN (1804-1855)

...when I look on you a moment, then can

I speak no more, but my tongue

falls silent, and at once a delicate flame

courses beneath my skin, and with my eyes

I see nothing, and my ears hum, and a wet sweat

bathes me, and a trembling seizes me all over....

SAPPHO (C.655-610 B.C.)

Oh, the comfort –
the inexpressible comfort,
of feeling safe with a person –
having neither to weigh thoughts
nor measure words,
but pouring them out.

DINAH MARIA MULOCK CRAIK
(1820-1887)

What happiness to be beloved!

There is only one happiness in life,
to love and be loved.

GEORGE SAND [AMANDINE AURORE LUCIE DUPIN] (1804-1876),
IN A LETTER TO LINA CALAMATTA

I am loved: a message clanging of a bell in silence.

JOYCE CAROL OATES, B.1938, FROM " HOW GENTLE"

To discover one is loved in return
– that is absolutely incredulity,
is overwhelming joy,
is peace beyond comprehension.

PAM BROWN, B.1928

and O, what bliss, ye gods, to love!

JOHANN WOLFGANG VON GOETHE (1749-1832)

*Love can surround in glory
the lives of little people.*

How bright,
how clear this light,
this love
that shines out
in a shadowed world.

PAM BROWN, B.1928

Nothing is sweeter than love,
Nothing stronger,
Nothing higher,
Nothing wider,
Nothing more pleasant
Nothing fuller or better in heaven or earth.

THOMAS Á KEMPIS (1379-1471), FROM "IMITATIO CHRISTI"

In the bits and pieces
of a person's life

A person's life isn't orderly,

it runs about all over the place,

in and out through time.

The present's hardly there;

the future doesn't exist.

Only love matters in the bits and pieces

of a person's life.

WILLIAM TREVOR, B.1928

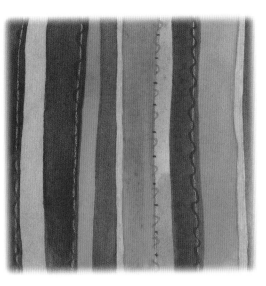

the games of love

It would be easier to count every grain of sand
across Africa, or to count the stars,
than to calculate the games of love you two will play.

CATULLUS (C.84-C.54 B.C.)

...my life, my all

Love conquers all things: let us too give in to love.

VIRGIL (70-19 B.C.), FROM "ECLOGUE", BK. X

Love so amazing,
so divine
Demands my soul,
my life, my all.

ISAAC WATTS (1674-1748)

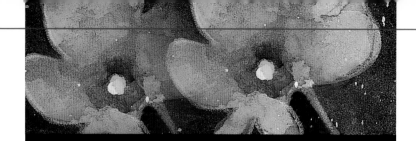

Above all she has
given me herself
to live for!
Her arms are able
to charm away
every care;
her words are my solace
and inspiration
and all because
her love is my life....

THOMAS WOODROW WILSON
(1856-1924),
TO HIS WIFE ELLEN

iridescent, deep, pulsing

I am writing to you, my pen dipped in the pine scent
of this afternoon, so that you can breathe the words
in and find the image I have for you in my heart.
The letters swim....
There are islands between the paragraphs.
Islands of green trees frothing out from bleached rock.
Further still await the satin mountains.
Feel the caress of their mystical invitation.
I am writing to you, while fish leap
between the commas and fullstops;
iridescent and curved like miniature sunbeams.
I hold a stone, a warm pulse in my hand
that contains the sun.
It is time itself, your time, my time.
I parcel it to you, inscribed with memories
that flow into deeper hues with each breath.

STEPHANIE JUNE SORRELL, B.1956

The sweetest joy,
the wildest woe is love.

PHILIP JAMES BAILEY (1816-1902),
FROM "FESTUSA: A LOVE AND GARDEN"

Who can give law to lovers?
Love is a greater law to itself.

BOETHIUS (C.480-524),
FROM "DE CONSOLATIONE PHILOSOPHIAE"

HE POURED SO GENTLY AND NATURALLY INTO MY LIFE

LIKE BATTER INTO A BOWL OF BATTER.

HONEY INTO A JAR OF HONEY.

THE CLEAREST WATER SINKING INTO SAND.

JUSTINE SYDNEY

while spring and summer sang

All are my blooms,
and all sweet blooms of love
To thee I gave while
spring and summer sang.

DANTE GABRIEL ROSSETTI
(1828-1882)

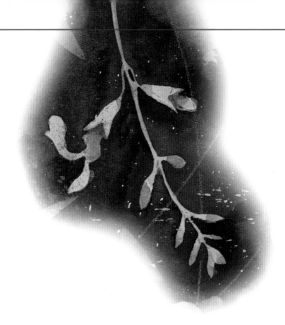

I will twine the white violet
and I will twine the delicate narcissus
with myrtle buds,
and I will twine the sweet crocus,
and I will twine therewithal
the crimson hyacinth,

Over the lovelocks
of her hair

and I will twine lovers' roses,
that on balsam-curled
Heliodora's temples
my garland may shed
its petals over the lovelocks
of her hair.

MELEAGER

LOVE

To love is
the great Amulet
that makes
this world a garden.

ROBERT LOUIS STEVENSON
(1850-1894)

To love is to take the greatest risk of all.
It is to give one's future and one's happiness
into another's hands.
It is to allow oneself to trust without reserve.

HELEN EXLEY

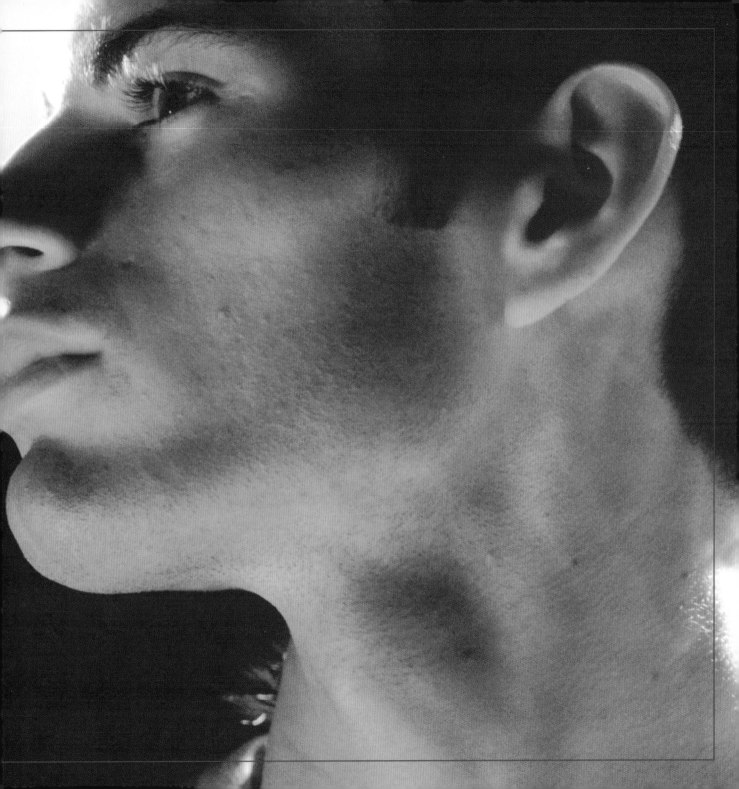

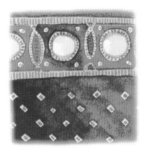

Sew a coat for my love

      take the sun for cloth

   cut the moon for lining

put the clouds for padding

    borrow the sea-spray for thread

  use the stars for buttons

    and make the buttonholes of me.

ARMENIAN FOLK SONG

Nobody else in the world

In love. She remembered the excitement of those days.
The sudden ecstasy of an unexpected telephone call.
The brilliance and beauty of the most mundane objects.
Laughter over nothing, shared across small candlelit tables;
walking together on sunlit pavements;
smelling lilac on a city street; driving in his car
down to the country, with the sun roof open
to the sky and a whole weekend ahead,
and the sensation that there was nobody in the world
but the two of them.

ROSAMUNDE PILCHER, B.1924, FROM "THE STONE BOY"

TAKE HIM AND CUT HIM OUT

IN LITTLE STARS,

AND HE WILL MAKE

THE FACE OF HEAVEN SO FINE

THAT ALL THE WORLD

WILL BE IN LOVE WITH NIGHT

AND PAY NO WORSHIP

TO THE GARISH SUN.

WILLIAM SHAKESPEARE (1564-1616),
FROM "ROMEO AND JULIET"

love's desires

Love has no other desire but to fulfil itself.

But if you love and must needs have desires,

let these be your desires:

To melt and be like a running brook that sings

its melody to the night.

To know the pain of too much tenderness.

To be wounded by your own understanding of love;

And to bleed willingly and joyfully.

To wake at dawn with a winged heart and give

thanks for another day of loving;

To rest at the noon hour and meditate love's ecstasy;

To return home at eventide with gratitude;

And then to sleep with a prayer for the beloved

in your heart and a song of praise upon your lips.

KAHLIL GIBRAN (1883-1931), FROM "THE PROPHET"

We love being in love, that's the truth on't.

WILLIAM MAKEPEACE THACKERAY (1811-1863)

I will love

In you are flowers and firelight, stars and songbirds,
the scent of summer, the stillness just before the dawn.
I will love you dancing, singing, reading,
making, planning, arguing.
I will love you cantankerous and tired,
courageous and in terror, joyful, fearful and triumphant.
I will love you through all weathers and all change.

PETER GRAY

you

Love is unselfish, understanding and kind,
for it sees with its heart and not with its mind.
Love is the answer that everyone seeks.
Love is the language that every heart speaks.
Love can't be bought, it is priceless and free....
Love, like pure magic, is a sweet mystery.

HELEN STEINER RICE

The heart has reasons
that reason does
not understand.

BLAISE PASCAL (1623-1662)

Love reaches out

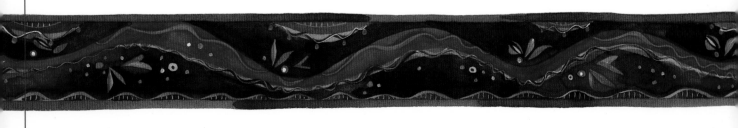

to shelter all

Love turns, changes, learns,

roots deep, discovers space and air.

Lifts leaves to sunlight and takes life from rain.

Yet shows its secret beauty

only when frost has stripped its branches.

Only shows endurance when storm tossed.

Love reaches out to shelter all.

PAM BROWN, B.1928

YOU FEEL THE SWEETNESS

[Love is]... something like the clouds
that were in the sky before the sun came out.
You cannot touch the clouds, you know;
but you feel the rain and know how glad
the flowers and the thirsty earth
are to have it after a hot day.
You cannot touch love either;
but you feel the sweetness
that it pours into everything.

ANNIE SULLIVAN (1866-1936)

Love is the life of the soul.
It is the harmony of the universe.

WILLIAM ELLERY CHANNING (1780-1842)

Love comforteth
like sunshine after rain.

WILLIAM SHAKESPEARE
(1564-1616)

You smile in passing, touch my shoulder.
I walk with you in the garden, sharing the last of the light,
the flickering of bats, the scent of roses.
We are at home in quietness.
Passion and the everyday flow from each other,
equal expressions of our love.

CHARLOTTE GRAY, B.1937

PEACE

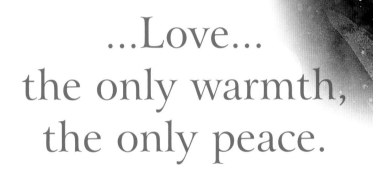

...Love...
the only warmth,
the only peace.

DELMORE SCHWARTZ
(1913-1966),
FROM "FOR THE ONE WHO WOULD TAKE
MAN'S LIFE IN HIS HANDS"

QUIETNESS

*A*ll loves lead
to the final love,
to the final stripping away
of the unreal selves,
to the true meeting....
Whenever it happened,
it was the true meeting,
the true marriage.

ANNE MORROW LINDBERGH
(1906-2001)

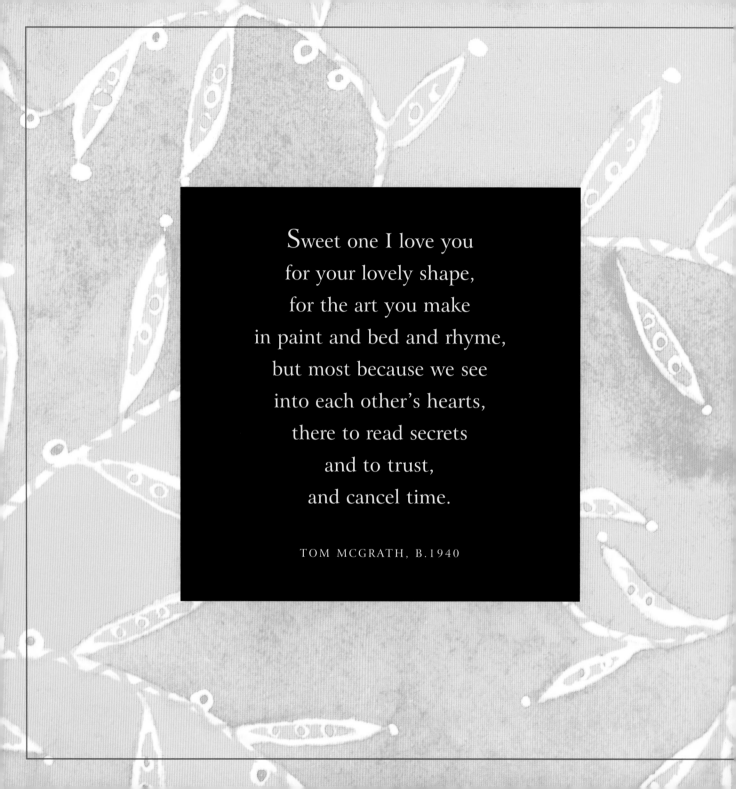

Sweet one I love you
for your lovely shape,
for the art you make
in paint and bed and rhyme,
but most because we see
into each other's hearts,
there to read secrets
and to trust,
and cancel time.

TOM MCGRATH, B.1940

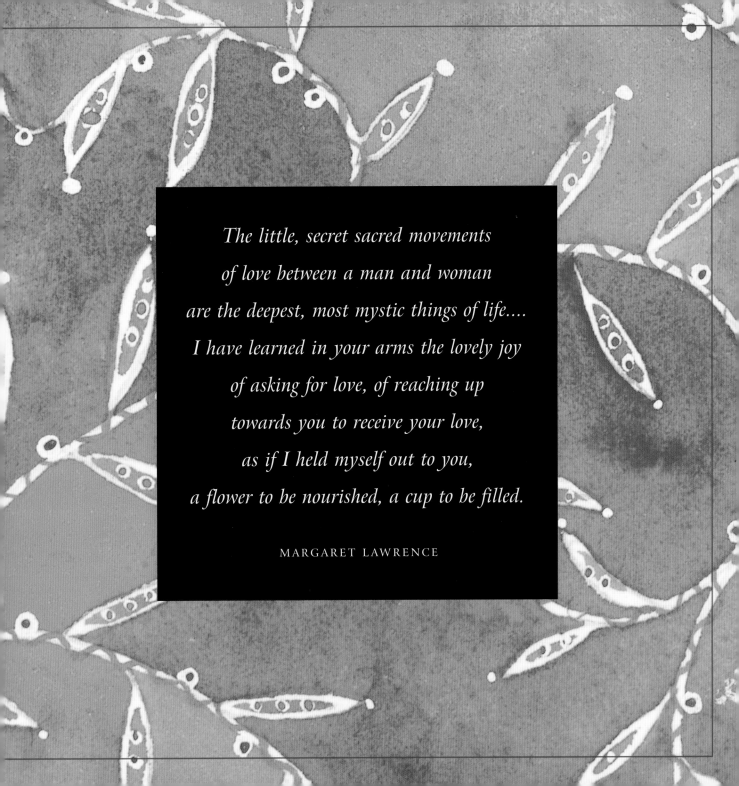

The little, secret sacred movements

of love between a man and woman

are the deepest, most mystic things of life....

I have learned in your arms the lovely joy

of asking for love, of reaching up

towards you to receive your love,

as if I held myself out to you,

a flower to be nourished, a cup to be filled.

MARGARET LAWRENCE

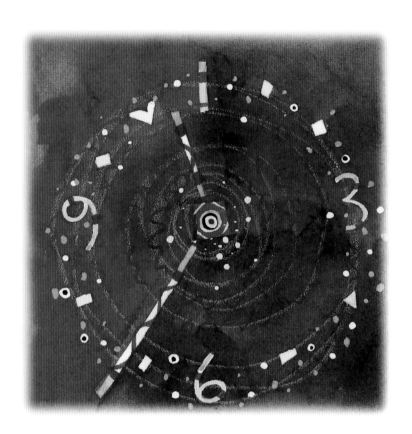

LOVE VANQUISHES TIME

Love vanquishes time. To lovers,

a moment can be eternity,

eternity can be the tick of a clock.

Across the barriers of time

and the ultimate destiny,

love persists for the home of the beloved,

absent or present,

is always in the mind and heart.

Absence does not diminish love.

MARY PARRISH
[MARGARET COUSINS],
B.1905,
FROM "MCCALLS" MAGAZINE

*N*ow you will feel no rain,
For each of you will be
shelter to the other.
Now you will feel no cold,
For each of you will be
warmth to the other.
Now there is no loneliness for you;
Now there is no more loneliness.
Now you are two persons
But there is one life before you.

APACHE BLESSING

Love is a plant of tenderest
growth: treat it well,
take thought for it
and it may grow strong
and perfume your whole life.

FRANK HARRIS (1856-1951)
TO RITA (ERIKA LORENZ)

And true love
holds with
gentle hands
The hearts that
it entwines.

AUTHOR UNKNOWN

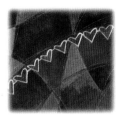

*L*ove has no other desire but to fulfil itself...
To melt and be like a running brook
that sings its melody to the night...
To wake at dawn with winged heart
and give thanks for another day of loving.

KAHLIL GIBRAN (1883-1931), FROM "THE PROPHET"

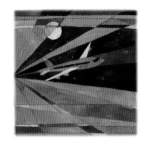

[Love is] born with the pleasure
of looking at each other, it is fed
with the necessity of seeing each other,
it is concluded with the impossibility
of separation!

JOSÉ MARTÍ Y PERÉZ (1853-1895), FROM "AMOR"

UNION

Two bodies,
Hearts beating in harmony.
A union,
Shared destiny,
A love embracing
eternity.

STUART AND LINDA MACFARLANE

Your love is comfort in sadness, quietness in tumult, rest in weariness, hope in despair.

MARION C. GARRETTY, B.1917

For one human being to love another human being:
that is perhaps the most difficult task
that has been entrusted to us, the ultimate task,
the final test and proof,
the work for which all other work is but preparation....

RAINER MARIA RILKE
(1875-1926)

THERE IS NO GRIEF, NO SORROW,
NO DESPAIR, NO LANGUOR, NO DEJECTION,
NO DISMAY, NO ABSENCE
SCARCELY CAN THERE BE,
FOR THOSE WHO LOVE AS WE DO.

WILLIAM WORDSWORTH
(1770-1850)

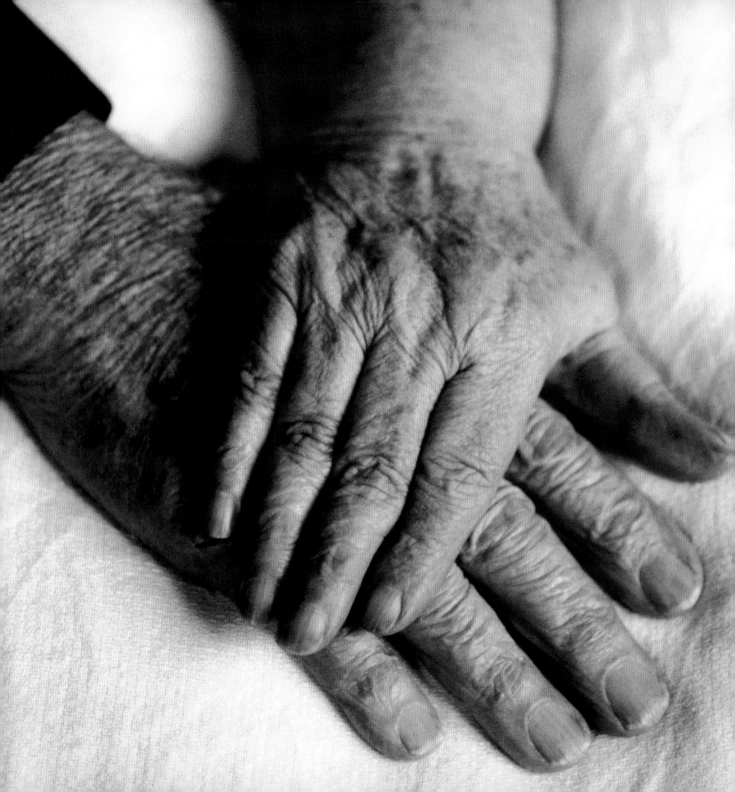

*I*s it so small a thing
To have enjoyed the sun,
To have lived light in the spring,
To have loved, to have thought,
to have done?

MATTHEW ARNOLD
(1822-1888)

Till a' the seas gang dry

As fair art thou, my bonnie lass,
So deep in love am I;
And I will love thee still, my dear,
Till a' the seas gang dry.

Till a' the seas gang dry, my dear,
And the rocks melt wi' the sun:
I will love thee still, my dear,
While the sands o' life shall run.

ROBERT BURNS (1759-1796)

I GAVE YOU ETERNITY

...I gave you the whole sun and stars to play with.
I gave you eternity in a single moment,
strength of the mountains
in one clasp of your arms,
and the volume of the seas
in one impulse of your soul...

GEORGE BERNARD SHAW (1856-1950)

Keres Indian Song

I add my breath to your breath
That our days may be long on the earth
That the days of our people may be long
That we may be one person
That we may finish our roads together.

that we may
finish our roads together

Sally has a smile I would accept
as my last view of earth.

smile

WALLACE STEGNER
(1909-1993)

Two things cannot alter,
Since Time was, nor today:
The flowing of water;
And Love's strange, sweet way.

JAPANESE LYRIC

ACKNOWLEDGEMENTS

The publishers are grateful for permission to reproduce copyright material. Whilst every effort has been made to trace copyright holders, the publishers would be pleased to hear from any not here acknowledged. FAIZ AHMED FAIZ: From *Last Night* by Faiz Ahmed Faiz, reproduced with permission of the Faiz estate; www.faiz.com. E.M. FORSTER: Extract from *Room with a View*, published by Edward Arnold, used with permission of The Provost and Scholars of King's College, Cambridge, The Society of Authors as the Literary Representatives of the estate of E.M. Forster, and Alfred A. Knopf, a division of Random House, Inc. KAHLIL GIBRAN: From *The Prophet* by Kahlil Gibran. Copyright 1923 by Kahlil Gibran and renewed 1951 by Administrators C.T.A. of Kahlil Gibran Estate and May G. Gibran. Reprinted by permission of Alfred A. Knopf, a division of Random House, Inc. THOMAS A KEMPIS: Six lines from *Imitatio Christi* by Thomas A Kempis, translated by Stephen Mitchell. From *"Into the Garden: A Wedding Anthology"* edited by Robert Hass and Stephen Mitchell. Copyright © 1993 by Robert Hass and Stephen Mitchell.

All rights reserved. Reprinted by arrangement with HarperCollins Publishers, Inc. TOM McGRATH: *Reasons* by Tom McGrath. Used by permission of the author. ROSAMUNDE PILCHER: From *The Stone Boy* Copyright © Rosamunde Pilcher, 1983. Reproduced by permission of Felicity Bryan and the author. CARL SANDBURG: *Under the Harvest Moon* from *"The Complete Poems of Carl Sandburg"*, copyright © 1970, 1969 by Lilian Steichen Sandburg, Trustee, reprinted by permission of Harcourt, Inc. GEORGE BERNARD SHAW: Extract from *Getting Married*. Used with permission of The Society of Authors, on behalf of the Bernard Shaw Estate. HELEN STEINER RICE: Used with permission of The Helen Steiner Rice™ Foundation, Cincinnati, Ohio, © 1970 The Helen Steiner Rice™ Foundation – All Rights Reserved. RABINDRANATH TAGORE: Extract from *Unending Love*, translated by William Radice.

Important copyright notice: Pam Brown, Helen Exley, Marion C. Garretty, Charlotte Gray, Peter Gray, Stuart & Linda Macfarlane are all © Helen Exley 2006.

LIST OF ILLUSTRATIONS

Helen Exley Giftbooks would like to thank the following organizations and individuals for permission to reproduce their pictures. Whilst every reasonable effort has been made to trace copyright holders, the publishers would be pleased to hear from any not here acknowledged.

Page 81 : The publishers have been unable to trace the copyright holders about this picture and would be grateful if they could contact us.

Pages 8/9, 19, 28, 66/67, 72/73, 76, 88, 102, 111, 120/121, 130/131, 133, 142, 149, 158, 160, 165, © SUPERSTOCK

Pages 45, 62, 92, © IMAGESTATE

Pages 58, 78, 82, 98, 113, 152, 168, © ZEFA

Page 12: © Reg Charity, CORBIS

Page 16/17: Gerhilde Skoberne, GETTY IMAGES

Page 22/23: J P Fruchet, GETTY IMAGES

Page 24/25: Ghislain & Marie David de Lossy, GETTY IMAGES

Page 32/33: Deborah Jaffe, GETTY IMAGES

Page 37: Noah Cross, GETTY IMAGES

Page 40: Denis Felix, GETTY IMAGES

Page 46/47: Dale Durfee, GETTY IMAGES

Page 53: Nick White, GETTY IMAGES

Page 68: Marcus Luconi, GETTY IMAGES

Page 96: © Charles Gupton, CORBIS

Page 107: Martin Barraud, GETTY IMAGES

Page 124: © DiMaggio, Kalish, CORBIS

Page 138/139: © Larry Williams, CORBIS

Page 155: © George Shelley, CORBIS

What is a Helen Exley Giftbook?

"Making a beautiful book like *The Great Gift of Love* is very much my life's work.
I spend years looking for the quotes to build my collections, and I'm always looking
for an elusive perfection," Helen Exley says. "It's like making a flower
arrangement with the most stunning flowers from everywhere in the world."
Helen sees her job as gathering the best words ever written, selecting the gems,
and then matching these with thoughtful illustrations to create
a truly beautiful gift. "It's a peaceful, happy job, because I have the choice of everything
ever written, everything ever painted, or photographed – plus the wonderful task
of bringing it all together. I try to create a gift that expresses
what we'd all love to be able to say ourselves, if only we had the time
to find the words. "The work is not work at all; it involves me reading about hope,
courage, friendship, love and family bonds. It's a great privilege."